Wise Words Series:

The Best Quotes from Oprah Winfrey

Compiled by: Alex Smith

Introduction

Oprah Winfrey is considered the most influential woman in the world. Rising up from a life of poverty, she has successfully been in the entertainment industry for over 30 years, and is globally known as an actress, philanthropist, writer, and media producer.

She is considered the richest African-American of the 20th century, and is also considered the greatest African American philanthropist in American history. Her television program, *The Oprah Winfrey Show*, which ran from 1986 to 2011, was the highest-rated talk show and held an international audience. Oprah launched her own cable network in 2011.

Over the years, Oprah has offered amazing insight and quotes through her various media outlets and public appearances: her television talk show, her magazine, keynote addresses at various events, YouTube videos, interviews and more.

This book contains over 250 of Oprah's most popular and inspirational quotes.

Compiled by Alex Smith

ISBN-13: 978-1976492372

Publish date: March 15, 2016

The Best Quotes from Oprah Winfrey

Do the one thing you think you cannot do. Fail at it. Try again. Do better the second time. The only people who never tumble are those who never mount the high wire. This is your moment. Own it.

The more you praise and celebrate your life, the more there is in life to celebrate.

What God intended for you goes far beyond anything you can imagine.

Where there is no struggle, there is no strength.

Surround yourself with only people who are going to lift you higher.

It isn't until you come to a spiritual understanding of who you are - not necessarily a religious feeling, but deep down, the spirit within - that you can begin to take control.

Lots of people want to ride with you in the limo, but what you want is someone who will take the bus with you when the limo breaks down.

Real integrity is doing the right thing, knowing that nobody's going to know whether you did it or not.

Turn your wounds into wisdom.

Passion is energy. Feel the power that comes from focusing on what excites you.

Follow your instincts. That's where true wisdom manifests itself.

Breathe. Let go. And remind yourself that this very moment is the only one you know you have for sure.

Be thankful for what you have; you'll end up having more. If you concentrate on what you don't have, you will never, ever have enough.

Cheers to a new year and another chance for us to get it right.

I feel that luck is preparation meeting opportunity.

What I know is, is that if you do work that you love, and the work fulfills you, the rest will come.

So go ahead. Fall down. The world looks different from the ground.

For every one of us that succeeds, it's because there's somebody there to show you the way out.

I don't think you ever stop giving. I really don't. I think it's an on-going process. And it's not just about being able to write a check. It's being able to touch somebody's life.

I am a woman in process. I'm just trying like everybody else. I try to take every conflict, every experience, and learn from it. Life is never dull.

I still have my feet on the ground, I just wear better shoes.

As you become more clear about who you really are, you'll be better able to decide what is best for you - the first time around.

I was raised to believe that excellence is the best deterrent to racism or sexism. And that's how I operate my life.

It does not matter how you came into the world, what matters is that you are here.

I believe that every single event in life happens in an opportunity to choose love over fear.

I have a lot of things to prove to myself. One is that I can live my life fearlessly.

I had no idea that being your authentic self could make me as rich as I've become. If I had, I'd have done it a lot earlier.

You know you are on the road to success if you would do your job, and not be paid for it.

What material success does is provide you with the ability to concentrate on other things that really matter. And that is being able to make a difference, not only in your own life, but in other people's lives.

You CAN have it all. You just can't have it all at once.

If you want to accomplish the goals of your life, you have to begin with the spirit.

When I look into the future, it's so bright it burns my eyes.

If you come to fame not understanding who you are, it will define who you are.

The thing you fear most has no power. Your fear of it is what has the power. Facing the truth really will set you free.

Understand that the right to choose your own path is a sacred privilege. Use it. Dwell in possibility.

I don't believe in failure. It is not failure if you enjoyed the process.

The biggest adventure you can ever take is to live the life of your dreams.

I've come to believe that each of us has a personal calling that's as unique as a fingerprint - and that the best way to succeed is to discover what you love and then find a way to offer it to others in the form of service, working hard, and also allowing the energy of the universe to lead you.

I trust that everything happens for a reason, even if we are not wise enough to see it.

Every day brings a chance for you to draw in a breath, kick off your shoes, and dance.

If friends disappoint you over and over, that's in large part your own fault. Once someone has shown a tendency to be self-centered, you need to recognize that and take care of yourself; people aren't going to change simply because you want them to.

One if the hardest things in life to learn are which bridges to cross and which bridges to burn.

You don't become what you want, you become what you believe.

You get to know who you really are in a crisis.

Challenges are gifts that force us to search for a new center of gravity. Don't fight them. Just find a new way to stand.

Your true passion should feel like breathing; it's that natural.

When you undervalue what you do, the world will undervalue who you are.

The reason I've been able to be so financially successful is my focus has never, ever for one minute been money.

The big secret in life is that there is no big secret. Whatever your goal, you can get there if you're willing to work.

With every experience, you alone are painting your own canvas, thought by thought, choice by choice.

Every time you state what you want or believe, you're the first to hear it. It's a message to both you and others about what you think is possible. Don't put a ceiling on yourself.

Create the highest, grandest vision possible for your life, because you become what you believe.

If you don't know what your passion is, realize that one reason for your existence on earth is to find it.

Think like a queen. A queen is not afraid to fail. Failure is another steppingstone to greatness.

If I lost control of the business, I'd lose myself--or at least the ability to be myself. Owning myself is a way to be myself.

Gratitude is the single greatest treasure I will take with me from this experience.

There is no such thing as failure. Failure is just life trying to move us in another direction.

I don't yell at people, I don't mistreat people. I don't talk down to people, so no one else in this building, in this vicinity, has the right to do it.

Use your life to serve the world, and you will find that it also serves you.

You are responsible for your life. If you're sitting around waiting on somebody to save you, to fix you, to even help you, you are wasting your time. Only you have the power to move your life forward.

I've talked to nearly 30,000 people on this show, and all 30,000 had one thing in common: They all wanted validation. They want to know, do you hear me? Do you see me? Does what I say mean anything to you? I would tell you that every single person you will ever meet shares that common desire.

Dogs are my favorite role models. I want to work like a dog, doing what I was born to do with joy and purpose. I want to play like a dog, with total, jolly abandon. I want to love like a dog, with unabashed devotion and complete lack of concern about what people do for a living, how much money they have, or how much they weigh. The fact that we still live with dogs, even when we don't have to herd or hunt our dinner, gives me hope for humans and canines alike

The great courageous act that we must all do, is to have the courage to step out of our history and past so that we can live our dreams.

Self-esteem comes from being able to define the world in your own terms and refusing to abide by the judgments of others.

You are responsible for your life. You can't keep blaming somebody else for your dysfunction. Life is really about moving on.

Doing the best at this moment puts you in the best place for the next moment.

Forgiveness is giving up the hope that the past could have been any different.

Only make decisions that support your self-image, self-esteem, and self-worth.

Every day brings a chance to live free of regret and with as much joy, fun, and laughter as you can stand.

The only people who never tumble are those who never mount the high wire.

The best thing about dreams is that fleeting moment, when you are between asleep and awake, when you don't know the difference between reality and fantasy, when for just that one moment you feel with your entire soul that the dream is reality, and it really happened.

I know for sure that what we dwell on is who we become.

It makes no difference how many peaks you reach if there was no pleasure in the climb.

Meditate. Breathe consciously. Listen. Pay attention. Treasure every moment. Make the connection.

You look at yourself and you accept yourself for who you are, and once you accept yourself for who you are you become a better person.

You have to find what sparks a light in you so that you in your own way can illuminate the world.

If you want your life to be more rewarding, you have to change the way you think.

To love yourself is a never-ending journey.

I believe the choice to be excellent begins with aligning your thoughts and words with the intention to require more from yourself.

In the mist of Difficulty lies Opportunity.

Your calling isn't something that somebody can tell you about. It's what you feel. It is the thing that gives you juice. The thing that you are supposed to do. And nobody can tell you what that is. You know it inside yourself.

Education is the key to unlocking the world, a passport to freedom.

You are where you are in life because of what you believe is possible for yourself.

My idea is to give hope, because where there is no hope, there is no vision, and where there is no vision, people will perish.

You aren't your past, you are the probability of your future.

The best of times is now.

I finally realized that being grateful to my body was key to giving more love to myself.

You are built not to shrink down to less but to blossom into more.

If you're going to binge, literature is definitely the way to do it.

Every one of us gets through the tough times because somebody is there, standing in the gap to close it for us.

We are not Human Beings experiencing spiritual lives, we are spiritual beings experiencing human lives.

You face the biggest challenge of all: to have the courage to seek your big dream regardless of what anyone says. You are the only person alive who can see your big picture and even you can't see it all.

Opportunity may knock only once but temptation leans on the door bell.

Difficulties come when you don't pay attention to life's whisper. Life always whispers to you first, but if you ignore the whisper, sooner or later you'll get a scream.

The happiness you feel is in direct proportion to the love you give.

You teach people how to treat you.

I've learned that you can't have everything and do everything at the same time.

Running is the greatest metaphor for life, because you get out of it what you put into it.

I choose to rise up out of that storm and see that in moments of desperation, fear, and helplessness, each of us can be a rainbow of hope, doing what we can to extend ourselves in kindness and grace to one another. And I know for sure that there is no them - there's only us.

I will tell you that there have been no failures in my life. I don't want to sound like some metaphysical queen, but there have been no failures. There have been some tremendous lessons.

Always take a stand for yourself, your values. You're defined by what you stand for.

I was once afraid of people saying, "Who does she think she is?" Now I have the courage to stand and say, "This is who I am."

What I know for sure is that what you give comes back to you.

Life is about growth and change. When you are no longer doing that — that is your whisper; that is your whisper that you are supposed to do something else.

When I didn't have friends, I had books.

The essential question is not, "How busy are you?' but 'What are you busy at?' 'Are you doing what fulfills you?"

Devote today to something so daring even you can't believe you're doing it.

I want every day to be a fresh start on expanding what is possible.

What other people label or might try to call failure, I have learned is just God's way of pointing you in a new direction.

Follow your feelings. If it feels right, move forward. If it doesn't feel right, don't do it.

You've got to follow your passion. You've got to figure out what it is you love--who you really are. And have the courage to do that. I believe that the only courage anybody ever needs is the courage to follow your own dreams.

The roles we play in each other's lives are only as powerful as the trust and connection between us--the protection, safety, and caring we are willing to share.

One of the greatest gifts you can give is your undivided attention.

If you neglect to recharge a battery, it dies. And if you run full speed ahead without stopping for water, you lose momentum to finish the race.

All pain is the same.

Connect. Embrace. Liberate. Love somebody. Just one person. And then spread that to two. And as many as you can. You'll see the difference it makes.

I would like to thank the people who've brought me those dark moments, when I felt most wounded, betrayed. You have been my greatest teachers.

What I love most about reading: It gives you the ability to reach higher ground, and keep climbing.

There is one irrefutable law of the universe: We are each responsible for our own life.

If you're holding anyone else accountable for your happiness, you're wasting your time. You must be fearless enough to give yourself the love you didn't receive.

The greatest discovery of all time is that a person can change his future by merely changing his attitude.
Know this for sure: When you get the chance, go for it.

Love is a lesson worth learning.

Beginning when we are girls, most of us are taught to deflect praise. We apologize for our accomplishments. We try to level the field with our family and friends by downplaying our brilliance. We settle for the passenger's seat when we long to drive. That's why so many of us have been willing to hide our light as adults. Instead of being filled with all the passion and purpose that enable us to offer our best to the world, we empty ourselves in an effort to silence our critics. The truth is that the naysayers in your life can never be fully satisfied. Whether you hide or shine, they'll always feel threatened because they don't believe they are enough. So stop paying attention to them. Every time you suppress some part of yourself or allow others to play you small, you are ignoring the owner's manual your Creator gave you. What I know for sure is this: You are built not to shrink down to less but to blossom into more. To be more splendid. To be more extraordinary. To use every moment to fill yourself up.

Life is full of many unpredictable changes. Let go of chaos yesterday; cheerfully live for today, and look forward to tomorrow with greater possibilities. It's our imperfections that make us perfect in our own unique ways.

Energy is the essence of life. Every day you decide how you're going to use it by knowing what you want and what it takes to reach that goal, and my maintaining focus.

What I find powerful is a person with the confidence to be her own self.

Improving your life doesn't have to be about changing everything – it's about making changes that count.

All stress comes from resisting what is.

You can either waltz boldly onto the stage of life and live the way you know your spirit is nudging you to, or you can sit quietly by the wall, receding into the shadows of fear and self-doubt.

There's a difference between thinking you deserve to be happy and knowing that you are worthy of being happy. Your being alive makes worthiness your birthright. You alone are enough.

Living in the moment brings you a sense of reverence for all of life's blessings.

I think that when you invite people to your home, you invite them to yourself.

After the hundreds of stories I've heard of atrocities around the globe, I know that if you're a woman born in the United States, you're one of the luckiest women in the world. Take your good fortune and lift your life to its highest calling. Understand that the right to choose your own path is a sacred privilege. Use it.

Do what you have to do until you can do what you want to do.

We are each responsible for our own life-no other person can be.

My approach to living with purpose has always been to create the life I want, one conscious decision at a time.

Before you agree to do anything that might add even the smallest amount of stress to your life ask yourself, "What is my truest intention?" Give yourself time to let a yes resound within you. When it's right, I guarantee that your entire body will feel it.

One of my greatest lessons has been to fully understand that what looks like a dark patch in the quest for success is the universe pointing you in a new direction. Anything can be a miracle, a blessing, an opportunity if you choose to see it that way.

The happiest people don't have the best of everything, they make the best of everything.

The struggle of my life created empathy - I could relate to pain, being abandoned, having people not love me.

Follow your passion. It will lead you to your purpose.

As long as other people's opinions matter more than your own, you're owned by them. You're not even free.

He who dies with the most toys is still dead.

I know for sure that you cannot give to everyone else and not give back to yourself. You will end up empty, or at best, less than what you can be for yourself and your family and your work. Replenish the well of yourself, for yourself.

Successful people never worry about what others are doing.

Become the change you want to see — those are words I live by. Instead of belittling, uplift.

Eat foods that make you thrive.

No matter what challenge you may be facing, you must remember that while the canvas of your life is painted with daily experiences, behaviors, reactions, and emotions, you're the one controlling the brush. If I had known this at 21, I could have saved myself a lot of heartache and self-doubt. It would have been a revelation to understand that we are all the artists of our own lives — and that we can use as many colors and brushstrokes as we like.

Truth allows you to live with integrity. Everything you do and say shows the world who you really are. Let it be the Truth.

I define joy as a sustained sense of well-being and internal peace - a connection to what matters.

Partake of some of life's sweet pleasures. And yes, get comfortable with yourself.

I've always known that life is better when you share it. I now realize it gets even sweeter when you expand the circle.

If a man wants you, nothing can keep him away. If he doesn't want you, nothing can make him stay.

Don't worry about being successful but work towards being significant and the success will naturally follow.

When people show you who they are, believe them!

I have a lot of things to prove to myself. One is that I can live my life fearlessly.

I believe that one of life's greatest risks is never daring to risk.

All of life is energy and we are transmitting it at every moment.

If you want to feel good, you have to go out and do some good.

It doesn't matter who you are, where you come from. The ability to triumph begins with you — always.

Books were my pass to personal freedom. I learned to read at age three, and there discovered was a whole world to conquer that went beyond our farm in Mississippi.

The true meaning of courage is to be afraid, and then, with your knees knocking and your heart racing, to step out anyway — even when that step makes sense to nobody but you. I know that's not easy. But making a bold move is the only way to truly advance toward the grandest vision the universe has for you.

Live from the heart of yourself. You have to make a living. I understand that. But, you also have to know what sparks the light in you so that you, in your own way, can illuminate the world.

You are responsible for your life, so don't wait for somebody else to fix you, to save you or complete you. JERRY MAGUIRE was just a movie. No one completes you.

We all know that we are better than the cynicism and the pessimism that is regurgitated throughout Washington and the 24-hour cable news cycle.

It doesn't matter how far you might rise. At some point, you are bound to stumble. If you're constantly pushing yourself higher and higher, the law of averages predicts that you will at some point fall. And when you do, I want you to remember this: There is no such thing as failure. Failure is just life trying to move us in another direction. Now, when you're down there in the hole, it looks like failure. When that moment comes, it's okay to feel bad for a little while. Give yourself time to mourn what you think you may have lost. But then, here's the key: Learn from every mistake, because every experience, particularly your mistakes, are there to teach you and force you into being more who you are.

The single most important lesson I learned in 25 years talking every single day to people, was that there's a common denominator in our human experience. The common denominator I found in every single interview is we want to be validated. We want to be understood.

I come from a people who have struggled and died in order to have a voice in this country. And I refused to be muzzled.

I never think about what I want. It's about what you want to give.

You cannot blame apartheid, your parents, your circumstances, because you are not your circumstances. You are your possibilities. If you know that, you can do anything.

I think if you believe in the awe and the wonder and the mystery, then that *is* what God is. That *is* what God is, not the bearded guy in the sky.

I know where my lane is, and I know how to stay in my lane. My lane is evolving the consciousness of people.

The thing that I do best is "Be Here. Be Now."

The key to realizing a dream is to focus not on success but on significance -- and then even the small steps and little victories along your path will take on greater meaning.

Not everyone can be famous but everyone can be great. Greatness is determined by service.

If you were born, there was a reason for you to be here.

Excellence is the best deterrent to sexism, so be excellent.

Because you were born, you are worthy!

Whatever has happened to you was also happening for you. There is no one thing that has ever happened in your life that was wasted. You were building strength, and strength times strength times strength times strength equals POWER.

Don't let anyone stop you from your life journey.

Align your personality with your purpose, and no one can touch you.

What am I hungry for? Well, I'm hungry to awaken and open people's hearts.

When you have reached the peak of a mountain top, you have absolutely no worries. But you have two choices: You can come down from the mountain and spend the rest of your days thinking it was so beautiful there, or you can create a vision, look upward, see the next mountain, and start the climb all over again.

That's what true leadership is — to be able to put whatever you're doing in a position that can sustain itself without you having to be the prominent force every day. You want to create an opportunity for other people.

The commonality in the human experience is the same. We have the same sorrows, and the same triumphs. Joy is joy is joy.

Every time you suppress some part of yourself or allow others to play you small, you are in essence ignoring the owner's manual your creator gave you and destroying your design.

I knew there was a way out. I knew there was another kind of life because I had read about it. I knew there were other places, and there was another way of being.

I don't think you ever stop giving. I really don't. I think it's an on-going process. And it's not just about being able to write a check. It's being able to touch somebody's life.

Free speech not only lives. It rocks! In the end, all you have is your reputation.

Shine within you so that it can shine on someone else. Let your light shine.

From you whose names I will never know, I learned what love is. And this show has been the great love of my life.

Everyone has a platform. Mine is a stage in a studio. Yours is wherever you are, with your own reach.

The chance to love and be loved exists no matter where you are.

Stop the crazy mind chatter in your head that tells you all the time that you are not good enough.

I think education is power. I think that being able to communicate with people is power. One of my main goals on the planet is to encourage people to empower themselves.

You cannot hate other people without hating yourself.

When ordinary people decide to do extraordinary things they transform their lives and the lives of others around them.

I didn't want to say "No" because I didn't want people to think I'm not nice. And that, to me, has been the greatest lesson of my life: to recognize that I am solely responsible for it, and not trying to please other people, and not living my life to please other people, but doing what my heart says all the time.

Keep a grateful journal. Every night, list five things that happened this day that you are grateful for. What it will begin to do is change your perspective of your day and your life. If you can learn to focus on what you have, you will always see that the universe is abundant; you will have more. If you concentrate on what you don't have, you will never have enough.

Every choice in life either moves you forward or keeps you stuck.

I don't have a lot of "I can't" inside me.

I have incredible stamina-- the what-do-I-got-that-they-ain't-got kind of stamina.

Don't back down just to keep the peace. Standing up for your beliefs builds self-confidence and self-esteem.

At the roll call of your life, at the end of your life, what really matters is who did you love and who did you offer love to.

Your job is to find your flow. This was a huge lesson for me. Everything else is gravy.

The greatest miracle is to still be alive.

Happiness is a living thing. You have to feed it.

This year I am choosing to live beyond my wildest dreams. I wonder where they'll take me.

Knowing your deepest intention can be your guiding force in the creation of a better life.

Getting my lifelong weight struggle under control has come from a process of treating myself as well as I treat others in every way.

You cannot live a brave life without disappointing some people. But those people who get disappointed- it's really okay- because the people who really care for you, the people who are rooting for your rise, will not be disappointed.

Whatever you fear most has no power - it is your fear that has the power. The thing itself cannot touch you. But if you allow your fear to seep into your mind and overtake your thoughts, it will rob you of your life.

The whole point of being alive is to evolve into the complete person you were intended to be.

What I know for sure is that it's only when you make the process your goal that the big dream can follow. That doesn't necessarily mean your process will necessarily lead you to wealth or fame. In fact, your dream may have nothing to do with tangible prosperity and everything to do with creating a life filled with joy, one with no regrets and a clear conscience.

I've learned that wealth is a tool that gives you choices, but it can't compensate for a life not fully lived and it certainly can't create a sense of peace within you.

In every aspect of our lives, we are always asking ourselves, how am I of value? What is my worth? Yet I believe that worthiness is our birthright.

Use what you have to run toward your best - that's how I now live my life.

Biology is the least of what makes someone a mother.

What we're all striving for is authenticity, a spirit-to-spirit connection.

There's no easy way out. If there were, I would have bought it. And believe me, it would be one of my favorite things!

Unless you choose to do great things with it, it makes no difference how much you are rewarded, or how much power you have.

You get in life what you have the courage to ask for.

Alone time is when I distance myself from the voices of the world so I can hear my own.

If your friends disappoint you over and over, that's in large part your own fault. Once someone has shown a tendency to be self-centered, you need to recognize that and take care of yourself; people aren't going to change simply because you want them to.

A clarity of intention helped me live a more fearless life.

Let excellence be your brand. When you are excellent, you become unforgettable.

Doing the right thing, even when nobody knows you're doing the right thing, will always bring the right thing back to you.

We can't become what we need to be by remaining what we are.

There is nothing worse than betraying yourself.

Don't settle for a relationship that won't let you be yourself.

Do not waste your time with people who have shown you they really mean no good for you.

Sometimes you find out what you are supposed to be doing by doing the things you are not supposed to do.

I want to be so full that I am overflowing with enough to share with everybody else. I'm going to own the fullness without ego, without arrogance, but with an amazing sense of gratitude.

The single greatest thing you can do to change your life today would be to start being grateful for what you have today.

What I know for sure is this: You are built not to shrink down to less, but to blossom into more. To be more splendid. To be more extraordinary. To use every moment to fill yourself up.

No experience is ever wasted. Everything has meaning.

No gesture is too small when done with gratitude.

Forgiveness is letting go so that the past does not hold you prisoner, does not hold you hostage.

Every life is a platform.

Nothing happens until you decide. Make a decision and watch your life move forward.

Some women have a weakness for shoes. I can go barefoot if necessary. I have a weakness for books.

Check your ego at the door and check your gut instead. Every right decision I have ever made has come from my gut.

If you are still breathing, you have a second chance.

You are awareness disguised as a human being.

Never for a moment allow your greatness to interfere with your goodness.

It is your life and it is worth risking everything to make it yours.

The life you want is waiting to rise up to meet you ... Will you accept it? Do you feel worthy enough to accept it?

True forgiveness is when you can say: Thank you for that experience.

What you put out is already on its way back to you.

If you feel like he is stringing you along, then he probably is. Don't stay because you think "it will get better." You'll be mad at yourself a year later for staying when things are not better. The only person you can control in a relationship is you.

That's what life is: an open door to all that is possible. And that's a powerful thing.

If you feel incomplete, you alone must fill yourself with love in all your empty, shattered spaces.

Have the boldness to tell yourself the truth – every bit of it.

No matter where you are on your journey, that's exactly where you need to be. The next road is always ahead.

Most of us are taught to deflect praise. We apologize for our accomplishments. We try to level the field with our family and friends by downplaying our brilliance. We settle for the passenger's seat when we long to drive…Instead of being filled with all the passion and purpose that enable us to offer our best to the world, we empty ourselves in an effort to silence our critics. The truth is that the naysayers in your life can never be fully satisfied. Whether you hide or shine, they'll always feel threatened because they don't believe they are enough.

I believe that everyone is a keeper of a dream – and by tuning into one another's secret hopes, we can become better friends, better partners, better parents, and better lovers.

Don't get confused between what people say you are and who you know you are.

If you want the best the world has to offer, offer the world your best.

Dream big – dream very big. Work hard – work very hard. And after you've done all you can, you stand, wait and fully surrender.

Passion whispers to you through your feelings, beckoning you toward your highest good.

Doubt means don't. Don't move. Don't answer. Don't rush forward.

We're all called. If you're here breathing, you have a contribution to make.

Happiness is a choice.

Growing up poor is fantastic because it makes you dream bigger.

I believe in the power of consistency, and a brand is consistency over time. I accept that. I am a brand.

Never again am I going to be used for someone else's agenda.

I am an energetic force, and everything I am putting out into the world is an energetic force.

The greatest calling is service.

In anybody's business, you're going to make mistakes. My feeling is- don't make worthless mistakes. Let every mistake move you forward.

Everybody has trials. Ask this question- what is it here to teach me? Because there is not one thing that is happening in your life that isn't there to give you information about how to move to the next level. What am I blind to that I'm not seeing? That is what trial is in your face for. And how can I use this to move myself forward? What is my role in it? What did I do to get here?

No experience is wasted. Everything that has ever happened to you has also happened for you.

Pay attention to your life, because your life is speaking to you- always- in all ways.

Printed in Great Britain
by Amazon

54356712R00030

Introduction

Welcome to the thrilling, high-octane world of Formula 1—where speed, precision, and cutting-edge technology collide in a spectacle unlike any other. From the roaring engines that echo across iconic circuits to the split-second decisions that define victory and defeat, Formula 1 is more than just a sport; it's a celebration of human ingenuity and relentless pursuit of perfection.

This book takes you on a journey behind the scenes, uncovering the quirks, triumphs, and jaw-dropping facts that make Formula 1 a global phenomenon. Did you know F1 cars can drive upside down? Or that pit stops can be completed in less time than it takes to blink? These are just a taste of the 101 strange but true stories waiting for you within these pages. Whether you're a die-hard fan or a curious newcomer, this collection of fascinating facts will deepen your appreciation for the world's fastest sport. So buckle up, hold tight, and get ready to discover the wild, wonderful, and often unbelievable truths of Formula 1. The race begins here!

Fact 1

Formula 1 cars generate so much downforce that they can theoretically drive upside down in a tunnel at speeds of 120 mph or more.

Fact 2

The steering wheels of modern F1 cars have over 20 buttons, dials, and switches, controlling everything from brake balance to radio communication.

Fact 3

An F1 car's tires lose about 0.5 kilograms of weight during a race due to wear and high temperatures.

Fact 4

Drivers experience up to 6G during braking, meaning their body feels six times its weight due to the force.

Fact 5

The Monaco Grand Prix has been held since 1929 and is one of the few F1 circuits where overtaking is extremely challenging.

Fact 6

F1 engines typically last around 1,000 kilometers before needing a replacement, emphasizing performance over longevity.

Fact 7

The average F1 pit stop takes just about 2 seconds, faster than the blink of an eye.

Fact 8

The highest speed ever recorded by an F1 car in a race was 372.6 km/h (231.5 mph) by Valtteri Bottas in 2016.

Fact 9

F1 drivers lose approximately 3 kilograms of body weight during a race due to sweat and dehydration.

Fact 10

The first-ever Formula 1 World Championship race was held at Silverstone, UK, in 1950.

Fact 11

In the 2011 Canadian Grand Prix, Jenson Button won despite making six pit stops and being in last place midway through the race.

Fact 12

The longest F1 race in history was the 2011 Canadian Grand Prix, which lasted over four hours due to heavy rain and red flags.

Fact 13

Ferrari is the only team to have competed in every Formula 1 season since the championship began in 1950.

Fact 14

F1 cars can accelerate from 0 to 100 mph and back to 0 in just under 4 seconds.

Fact 15

A Formula 1 car's engine can reach up to 15,000 revolutions per minute (RPM), far higher than a typical road car.

Fact 16

The Pirelli tires used in F1 are designed to operate at temperatures of up to 120°C (248°F).

Fact 17

The Singapore Grand Prix, introduced in 2008, was the first-ever night race in Formula 1 history.

Fact 18

An F1 car's fuel tank can hold around 110 kilograms of fuel, enough to last an entire race under strict fuel management.

Fact 19

Each F1 car is made up of approximately 80,000 individual components, requiring precise assembly for optimal performance.

Fact 20

The average cost of a single F1 car is around $12 million, including research and development.

Fact 21

F1 teams employ around 1,000 people each, working on everything from car design to race strategy.

Fact 22

The shortest F1 circuit is the Monaco Grand Prix, measuring just 3.337 kilometers (2.074 miles) per lap.

Fact 23

The safety car, introduced in 1973, helps slow down the race during dangerous conditions to ensure driver safety.

Fact 24

Wind tunnels are extensively used by F1 teams to perfect the aerodynamics of their cars.

Fact 25

In 2005, the United States Grand Prix at Indianapolis saw only six cars start the race due to tire safety concerns.

Fact 26

The "halo" device, introduced in 2018, has saved multiple drivers from serious injury by protecting their heads from debris.

Fact 27

F1 cars can reach a speed of 0-60 mph in approximately 2.6 seconds, faster than most supercars.

Fact 28

The Australian Grand Prix is traditionally the first race of the F1 season, though it has been moved in some years.

Fact 29

A single F1 tire costs about $2,700, and teams use up to 13 sets per car during a race weekend.

Fact 30

Michael Schumacher holds the record for the most consecutive World Championships, winning five in a row from 2000 to 2004.

Fact 31

The fastest pit stop in F1 history was performed by Red Bull Racing in 2019, changing all four tires in just 1.82 seconds.

Fact 32

The Baku City Circuit in Azerbaijan features the longest straight on the F1 calendar, measuring 2.2 kilometers (1.37 miles).

Fact 33

Formula 1 cars can go from 200 mph to a complete stop in just 4 seconds, showcasing incredible braking power.

Fact 34

The "Constructors' Championship" was introduced in 1958, allowing teams to compete for a title alongside the drivers.

Fact 35

A Formula 1 car's cockpit is so small that drivers often have custom-molded seats to fit them perfectly.

Fact 36

Rain tires, also known as "wet tires," have grooves that help channel water away to maintain grip on wet tracks.

Fact 37

The Circuit de Spa-Francorchamps in Belgium is famous for its challenging Eau Rouge and Raidillon corner combination.

Fact 38

Lewis Hamilton has the most pole positions in F1 history, achieving over 100 during his career.

Fact 39

The first turbocharged car to win an F1 race was the Renault RS01, achieving victory in 1979.

Fact 40

In 2021, Max Verstappen won the World Championship after a dramatic final-lap battle with Lewis Hamilton in Abu Dhabi.

Fact 41

The KERS (Kinetic Energy Recovery System) introduced in 2009 stores energy during braking to provide extra power boosts.

Fact 42

F1 drivers are required to weigh themselves before and after races to monitor hydration and body fluid loss.

Fact 43

The "Undercut" strategy involves pitting earlier than competitors to gain time on fresh tires and overtake them when they pit.

Fact 44

The Circuit Gilles Villeneuve in Canada is known for the "Wall of Champions," which has ended the races of many F1 legends.

Fact 45

The youngest driver to start an F1 race is Max Verstappen, who debuted at 17 years and 166 days in 2015.

Fact 46

The rearview mirrors on F1 cars are specifically designed to reduce drag while providing clear visibility for drivers.

Fact 47

Sebastian Vettel holds the record for the most consecutive race wins in a single season, with nine in 2013.

Fact 48

The Circuit of the Americas in Austin, Texas, features a unique uphill start leading into a sharp hairpin turn.

Fact 49

F1 cars are equipped with advanced telemetry systems that transmit data in real time to the teams during races.

Fact 50

The "DRS" (Drag Reduction System) allows drivers to adjust their rear wings to reduce drag and increase speed for overtaking.

Fact 51

In 1992, Nigel Mansell clinched the F1 title with five races remaining, one of the earliest championship victories.

Fact 52

Formula 1 drivers train their neck muscles intensively to handle high G-forces during turns and braking.

Fact 53

The Indianapolis 500 was part of the F1 calendar from 1950 to 1960 but was dominated by American drivers.

Fact 54

F1 helmets weigh about 1.25 kilograms and are designed to withstand impacts of up to 225 km/h.

Fact 55

Mercedes AMG Petronas won seven consecutive Constructors' Championships from 2014 to 2020.

Fact 56

The "Parc Fermé" rules restrict changes to the cars between qualifying and the race to maintain fairness.

Fact 57

Honda, which first entered F1 in 1964, withdrew several times before returning as an engine supplier.

Fact 58

F1 uses over 500 sensors on a car to monitor performance and conditions in real time.

Fact 59

The "Formula" in Formula 1 refers to the set of rules to which all participants and cars must adhere.

Fact 60

The Circuit de Monaco has the slowest corner in F1, taken at just 48 km/h (30 mph).

Fact 61

Juan Manuel Fangio won five F1 World Championships during the 1950s, a record that stood for decades.

Fact 62

Some F1 teams spend over $400 million annually on their racing programs.

Fact 63

The "dirty air" effect behind an F1 car reduces the aerodynamic efficiency of following cars.

Fact 64

The Spanish Grand Prix is one of the oldest F1 events, dating back to 1913.

Fact 65

Each F1 car is hand-assembled, and building one takes approximately 2,000 man-hours, with precise attention to detail for optimal performance.

Fact 66

F1 teams test their cars in wind tunnels at speeds of over 300 km/h (186 mph) to simulate real-world race conditions and optimize aerodynamics.

Fact 67

The F1 World Championship has had a total of 33 different countries host a race since the series began.

Fact 68

The Italian Grand Prix, held at Monza, is one of the oldest and most prestigious races in F1, often called the "Temple of Speed."

Fact 69

Drivers are required to wear a HANS (Head and Neck Support) device, which reduces the risk of neck injuries in high-speed crashes.

Fact 70

The most successful F1 driver of all time is Lewis Hamilton, with a total of 7 World Championships, tying with Michael Schumacher.

Fact 71

F1 cars are capable of generating enough downforce to drive upside down, theoretically reaching speeds as low as 60 mph to maintain this effect.

Fact 72

The F1 calendar has featured over 70 different circuits, with a range of challenges, from street races to purpose-built tracks.

Fact 73

F1 cars use special high-performance fuel, which is different from the fuel found in regular road cars, ensuring maximum efficiency and power.

Fact 74

Fernando Alonso became the youngest double world champion in F1 history, winning back-to-back titles in 2005 and 2006.

Fact 75

The Pirelli tires used in F1 have a lifespan of only a few laps in some cases, requiring drivers to change them several times during a race.

Fact 76

The "Red Bull Racing" team pioneered the use of a "double diffuser" in 2009, which was later banned but led to increased aerodynamic efficiency.

Fact 77

In 1994, the F1 community suffered a massive blow when Ayrton Senna, one of the sport's most iconic figures, tragically died during the San Marino Grand Prix.

Fact 78

Formula 1 tracks feature a variety of surfaces, with some parts of the circuit being more abrasive than others, affecting tire wear.

Fact 79

F1 drivers communicate with their teams through radio messages, and some of the most famous quotes have become part of F1 history, such as "Box, box, box" for pit stops.

Fact 80

The F1 "pit wall" is where the race strategists, engineers, and team principal sit, making crucial decisions during a race using live telemetry data.

Fact 81

The 2021 Abu Dhabi Grand Prix marked one of the most dramatic title deciders in history, with Max Verstappen winning his first championship in controversial circumstances.

Fact 82

F1 cars are fitted with a fire suppression system, which can be activated manually or automatically in the event of a fire during a race.

Fact 83

Formula 1 cars can produce up to 1,000 horsepower, with a combination of internal combustion engines and hybrid systems contributing to this immense power.

Fact 84

An F1 car's brakes are made from carbon composite material, which can withstand temperatures of over 1,000°C (1,832°F).

Fact 85

The Monaco Grand Prix is one of the few races where qualifying results can be as important as the race itself due to the track's difficulty and narrow nature.

Fact 86

The "Brawn GP" team, formed after Honda's departure in 2008, won both the Drivers' and Constructors' Championships in 2009, despite being a new team.

Fact 87

F1 races are broadcast in over 200 countries, with millions of fans around the world tuning in to watch every race.

Fact 88

The fastest F1 car ever made in terms of lap time was the 2004 Ferrari F2004, which dominated the season and helped Michael Schumacher secure another World Championship.

Fact 89

F1 drivers are required to have a superlicense, which is a qualification that ensures they are experienced enough to compete in the sport.

Fact 90

Formula 1 cars feature "DRS zones" on certain tracks, where drivers can use a movable rear wing to reduce drag and increase speed, especially for overtaking.

Fact 91

A modern F1 car can generate over 5,000 newtons of downforce at top speed, enough to push the car onto the track like a vacuum.

Fact 92

The "fastest lap" in an F1 race is usually set towards the end of the race, when the car is at its lightest after consuming most of its fuel.

Fact 93

The 2020 F1 season saw the introduction of virtual races, where professional drivers competed in simulated races during the COVID-19 pandemic.

Fact 94

F1 cars are equipped with an array of sensors, including GPS, to provide live information about the car's position, speed, and condition during the race.

Fact 95

F1 pit crews work in perfect harmony, with each crew member performing a specialized task, from tire changes to wing adjustments, in just a few seconds.

Fact 96

The "Speed Trap" at certain F1 circuits measures the maximum speed reached by a car during the weekend, often capturing speeds of over 350 km/h (217 mph).

Fact 97

At the British Grand Prix, some fans traditionally wave "Union Jack" flags in tribute to local hero Lewis Hamilton, particularly after his wins.

Fact 98

The official F1 safety car has evolved over time, with the Mercedes-AMG GT being one of the most iconic models to be used in recent years.

Fact 99

Many F1 drivers practice with simulators to prepare for races, simulating different weather conditions, tire wear, and track layouts to perfect their strategies.

Fact 100

The 2012 Brazilian Grand Prix saw one of the most dramatic title deciders, with Sebastian Vettel clinching his third consecutive championship by just four points.

Fact 101

Formula 1 remains one of the most prestigious and technical motorsports in the world, with advancements in technology, safety, and racing strategies pushing the boundaries of speed and precision year after year.